MEET THE
MEDIEVALS

Liz Miles

Gareth Stevens
PUBLISHING

Please visit our website, **www.garethstevens.com**. For a free color catalog of all our high-quality books, call toll free 1-800-542-2595 or fax 1-877-542-2596.

Miles, Liz.
Meet the Medievals / by Liz Miles.
p. cm. — (Encounters with the past)
Includes index.
ISBN 978-1-4824-0890-4 (pbk.)
ISBN 978-1-4824-0891-1 (6-pack)
ISBN 978-1-4824-0889-8 (library binding)
1. Civilization, Medieval — Juvenile literature. 2. Middle Ages — Juvenile literature.
I. Miles, Liz. II. Title.
D117.M55 2015
940.1—d23

First Edition

Published in 2015 by
Gareth Stevens Publishing
111 East 14th Street, Suite 349
New York, NY 10003

Copyright © Arcturus Holdings Limited

Editors: Joe Harris and Nicola Barber
Design: Elaine Wilkinson
Cover design: Elaine Wilkinson

Cover pictures Shutterstock: Shutterstock: Conwy Castle Magdanatka, medieval girl Darja Vorontsova, coin t50, helmet Ivan Smuk.

Picture acknowledgements: Alamy: p9 bottom Cotswolds Photo Library; p19 bottom Steve Sant; p26 Ivy Close Images. The Bridgeman Art Library: p4 pilgrim badge Museum of London, UK; p11 top Bibliotheque de L'Arsenal, Paris, France/Archives Charmet; p11 bottom British Library, London, UK/© British Library Board. All Rights Reserved; p19 top Musee National du Moyen Age et des Thermes de Cluny, Paris. Getty: p27 top De Agostini, p27 bottom. Guarderobe (www.guarderobe.co.uk): p23 top. iStockphoto: p22 Juanmonino. Shutterstock: p4 background Khunaspix, top inset McCarthy's PhotoWorks, coins left KA Photography KEVM111, middle Sponner, right t50, pouch Scott Rothstein; pp5, 22-3 and 28 Gail Johnson; pp6-7 and 7 bottom Gail Johnson; p6 and title page Sergey Kamshylin; p7 top Radu Razvan; p8 Kirill Livshitskiy; p9 top Daniele Pietrobelli; p10 Radu Razvan; pp12-13 Unholy Vault Designs; p12 Radu Razvan; p13 and contents McCarthy's PhotoWorks; p13 bottom FotograFFF; pp14-15 Capture Light; p14 Alastair Wallace; p15 top Anneka; pp16-17 Christian Delbert; p16 McCarthy's PhotoWorks; p17 top defpicture; p17 bottom Radu Razvan; pp18-19 Lincoln Rogers; p18 and title page coxy58; pp20-21 Dawid Lech; p20, 21 and title page Natali Glado; p21 bottom Igor Sokolov (breeze); p23 bottom alb_photo; pp24-5 Upthebanner; pp24 and 25 top Radu Razvan; p25 bottom McCarthy's PhotoWorks; pp26-7 Claudio Divizia; p28 Salajean; p29 Gail Johnson. Wikimedia Commons: pp8-9 Cruccone; pp10-11 Andrew Dunn; p15 bottom Adrian Pingstone.
All rights reserved. No part of this book may be reproduced in any form without permission from the publisher, except by reviewer.

Printed in the United States of America

CPSIA compliance information: Batch CS15GS: For further information contact Gareth Stevens, New York, New York at 1-800-542-2595.

Contents

Into the Past

It's nighttime and you are having a vivid dream – you are a medieval noble watching a knight at a tournament. At school you have been learning all about medieval Britain – how the poor and the wealthy lived, and the exploits of the knights.

Suddenly, you wake up. You sit up and stare. At the end of your bed, an old wooden door has appeared. Trembling, you get up, and lift the iron latch to open it. You walk into a small, candlelit room. Beside an open hearth on the stone floor, there is a simple bed made of straw. On a wooden table, there's a handwritten note.

The face of Thomas Becket, Archbishop of Canterbury, stares out of this pilgrim badge. Becket was made a saint after his murder in Canterbury Cathedral in 1170.

YOUR MISSION

Your journey starts here. You are about to enter a medieval town. It's the winter of 1294 CE, during the reign of Edward I. Your mission is to meet people and find out about their lives. These clothes will disguise you as a servant. Your mission will last six hours.

Quickly, you choose some clothes from the pile. You wrap a cloak around your shoulders and pull on some leather shoes. There are some coins for you too.

Another door in the room creaks open. Shouts from street-sellers and bargaining shoppers and the clip-clop of horses' hooves fill your ears. Then there's a horrible smell of open drains and rotting garbage. Holding your breath, you step outside.

The Servant's Errands

You walk into a crowded street under a high stone wall. Suddenly a boy runs into you, knocking you over. He helps you up, apologizing. He tells you that he is a servant from the castle. He's in a rush because he's running some urgent errands for his squire – there's a big tournament starting in just a few hours. You offer to help, and he quickly accepts. He sets off and you follow, asking questions.

WHAT IS A SQUIRE?

A squire is a boy who is training to be a knight. My squire comes from a wealthy family but he lives away from home, in the castle here. He works for one of the knights. He is learning how to fight, to ride a horse and hunt. But he can't become a knight until he's shown courage on a battlefield.

WHO ELSE LIVES IN THE CASTLE?

There's the baron and his wife, and a few other knights with their families, squires, and pages. The baron is the boss, unless the king visits. There are lots of workers in the castle – grooms, blacksmiths, soldiers, kitchen maids, and servants. Sometimes we have visiting entertainers, such as mummers and troubadours – that's fun!

A troubadour was a musician who traveled from place to place, singing and playing for a living.

WHY IS THERE A WALL AROUND THIS TOWN?

It's to keep the baron and his court safe, and keep rebels and invaders out. Soldiers guard the walls from the battlements and keep watch from the towers. There are 21 towers! The walls also stop farmers and peasants from coming into the town without paying at the gates. The town traders and craftsmen don't like competition from outsiders.

A Wool Merchant

The servant's first stop is at the wool merchant's shop. The squire's doublet was torn in a fight, so he has to buy cloth for a new one. You both wait while the well-dressed merchant examines some raw wool from a peasant woman's cart. He haughtily shakes his head, then tosses the wool to the ground. She gathers it up, muttering angrily. While the merchant measures out cloth for the squire, you ask him some questions.

WHY DIDN'T YOU BUY THE WOMAN'S WOOL?

It wasn't good enough. As a member of the Merchant Wool Guild I know what standard of wool to accept and the right price. The peasant farmer's wool was too coarse and too expensive. I wish these folk from small farms weren't allowed into the town.

WHAT DOES THE GUILD DO?

The guild looks after its members. We keep outsiders like that woman away, and we buy our wool from the farmers we trust. We like to keep control of our trade. But if any of our members need help, we have a fund to support them. I'm proud to be in a town with so many fine guilds for our craftsmen, such as the spinners and stonemasons.

Spinning woolen thread from raw wool.

WHERE DO YOU MEET?

We meet at our guildhall. Thanks to the clever dealings of our guild master, we raised enough money to build a large hall in the market square. You'll see the guild's coat of arms above the door. I must hurry there now … the guild's court has to decide how to punish a member who's been selling bad-quality wool.

A brass memorial to a wealthy wool merchant.

Talking to the Leper

After paying for the cloth, the servant hurries you towards his next errand – at the blacksmith's. As you wait for a cart to pass, you pause to give a coin to a beggar. To your surprise, the servant pulls you away, and whispers, "Leave him alone! He has leprosy!" But you tell the servant to go on without you – you want to talk to the man.

DO YOU LIVE IN THIS TOWN?

I've lived here for years, but now that I'm ill, I'll have to leave. Begging is getting too risky – it's not allowed and I'll be thrown in the stocks if I'm caught. I wish I could earn money for food, but no one will give me any work. People are too scared of me, and of catching my disease.

WHERE WILL YOU GO?

A leper begging in the street.

There's a leper hospital outside the town walls, a few miles from here. The monks there will look after me. The hospital is a bit like a hostel for all sorts of people who are ill. The monks believe that because we suffer on earth, lepers like me will go straight to heaven when we die.

WHY DON'T THE TOWNSPEOPLE HELP YOU?

Some people believe that illness is a sign of sin. They don't want me to get near them in case my sin makes them unclean. Many people are just afraid of catching my disease. I have heard that in some parts of the country lepers are made to wear bells as a warning, so that people can run away as they approach. But I'm not sinful – I'm just ill.

A Visit to the Blacksmith

Y ou give another coin to the leper before running to catch up with the servant at the forge. The squire's sword was damaged during a practice fight, so the blacksmith is making a new one. You wait, sweating in the heat of the fire, while he finishes beating the iron blade. Then you ask him some questions.

HOW DO YOU MAKE A SWORD?

I heat the metal in this furnace. The fire has to be hot enough to make the metal soft and workable. It's very hot, dirty work! I use a hammer to shape and flatten the metal. Beating the metal into shape takes a lot of strength. I use rasps and files to smooth rough edges. Daggers are quicker to make than swords. But my bestsellers are the blades for long weapons like spears and glaives.

DO YOU MAKE ARMOR AS WELL?

The armorers at the castle make most of the plate armor, but I sometimes have to repair it. I can bang dents out of a breastplate, or weld patches over holes in the armor. I don't mend chain mail though – I haven't got the patience to make and link all those tiny rings!

WHAT ELSE DO YOU MAKE?

I make everything that people need – from horseshoes to spoons, cooking pots to door hinges. For the carpenters and stonemasons, I make tools like axes, chisels, and mallets. For the castle folk I make keys, chains, locks, and knives. I helped to make the castle's portcullis, too.

A blacksmith's tools.

A Monk at the Drawbridge

Clutching the heavy new sword and the cloth, you and the servant head for the castle. As you cross the drawbridge, you trip and drop the parcel of cloth. A monk stops to help you pick it up. The monk is on his way into the castle, too. As you wait for the soldiers to raise the portcullis, you ask the monk a few questions.

WHERE ARE YOU FROM?

I'm from a monastery not far from this town. I work as a scribe in the monastery. Today I'm bringing a religious manuscript to the baron. It's very precious – it took weeks for me to write it and the illuminator to illustrate it. Some of the lettering and miniature paintings are decorated with real gold.

WHAT DO YOU BELIEVE IN?

When I became a monk, I promised to follow a life of poverty, to obey my leaders, and never to marry. I believe that hard work and some discomfort is the way to God. Eight times every day we go to pray in the monastery church. We spend a lot of time reading and praying, but we also have to work hard.

WHAT IS IT LIKE TO LIVE IN A MONASTERY?

We grow all our own food and we look after the monastery. We have two simple meals a day. I hardly ever leave the monastery, so being permitted to travel to the castle is unusual for me. My work as a scribe is in praise of God. And like many monks, I also help to care for the poor and the sick people who come to our monastery for help.

A Bible with decorated lettering.

The Tired Kitchen Maid

Once inside the busy castle walls, the servant takes you to the kitchen in search of food. The vast smoky room is a hive of activity: iron cauldrons bubbling over a huge fire, servants chopping vegetables and turning a spit, maids washing pots and sliding bread into a cave-like oven. In the doorway, you find a tired young maid, secretly resting. You stop to talk to her.

WHAT SORT OF MEAL ARE YOU PREPARING?

It's a banquet – there's so much to do! For the high table, there's a roasted swan, other cooked meats, pies, sauces, fruit tarts, and jellies colored with saffron and cinnamon. For the low tables, there are the usual bread trenchers and some meat, fish, and pottage.

WHAT KITCHEN TOOLS DO YOU USE?

We've got stone pestles and mortars for grinding up food, wooden pots for mixing, clay pots to make pies, and metal knives and spoons. The baron and his nobles have silverware to eat their food. I wash the pots in a stone sink and I use sand to scrub off the grease.

A pestle and mortar.

HOW DO YOU STOP THE FOOD FROM GOING BAD?

We keep things cool in the pantry. It's got thick stone walls, and it's always cold in there! The meats are usually salted, dried, or smoked so they don't go rotten. If food does go bad we make it tastier by adding spices. We can't use too many spices though – they are very expensive. They come from faraway Eastern lands by ship.

The Noblewoman

While you were talking to the maid, the servant found out that the squire is with his mother. She is a noblewoman who is visiting the castle for the tournament. The servant guides you up a narrow, winding staircase to her rooms in the tower. While the squire examines his new sword, and feels the quality of the cloth, you ask the noblewoman a few questions about her life.

WHERE DO YOU LIVE?

I live in a manor not far from here. It's a good-sized estate, with plenty of villagers to work the land. I'm visiting the castle with my husband because he's one of the knights in the tournament. It's a chance to see my son, too. I miss him now that he lives away from home, but in order to be a knight he must learn about life in the castle.

WHAT'S LIFE AT THE MANOR LIKE?

As lord of the manor, my husband governs the village and owns the land. The land is farmed by peasants. My husband's reeve checks the peasants' farmwork and his bailiff makes sure they pay their rent. Most of the peasants give us part of their crops as rent. I have to organize the servants in the manor house. We're often out hunting too, with our hounds and hawks.

A medieval nobleman with his servants.

HOW MANY CHILDREN DO YOU HAVE?

Sadly, two of my children died when they were tiny babies. I have a daughter who stays with me or with her nurse. She is learning to embroider, and to read so that she can read her prayers and the Bible. I hope my son, the squire, will soon be a knight.

A young squire learns how to handle a sword.

At the Tournament

A noise from outside tells you that the tournament is about to begin. The squire runs to attend to his knight. You race after him, down to the courtyard. You watch as two horses charge towards each other, each ridden by a helmeted knight with a long lance. Another knight is standing beside you, waiting for his turn to joust, so you ask him a few questions.

HOW LONG DID IT TAKE FOR YOU TO BECOME A KNIGHT?

I came to this castle at the age of seven to serve as a squire's page. I learned how to fight and ride a horse. At 12, I became a squire and served a knight. In the castle I was taught the values of chivalry – to protect the weak, to honor womenfolk, and to be courteous and true. But it was only later, when I proved my bravery, that I was knighted.

HAVE YOU FOUGHT IN ANY REAL BATTLES?

My father died on a battlefield as a Crusader – he went with many other knights to battle for the Christian faith far away in the Holy Land. I was knighted after a battle in 1265. We were defending Edward, now king of England, against a rebellious earl and his barons – and we won.

WHAT ARE YOUR FAVORITE WEAPONS?

I prefer to keep the enemy at a good distance with a pole weapon, like a glaive. If I am pushed off my horse, I use a double-edged sword – it's good for fighting with a single hand, while holding a shield in the other. But faced with someone in heavy armor, I'd choose a heavy mace to swing hard at them.

The Doctor's Remedies

Your conversation with the knight is interrupted by a crash and a scream – one of the jousting knights has been knocked off his horse. The knight is carried away for treatment and you decide to follow. You notice a man with a bag who must be the doctor. You ask him some questions as servants remove the knight's armor and try to make him comfortable.

WHAT'S IN YOUR BAG?

There are herbs such as marjoram that I apply to cuts and bruises. I have other herbs, spices, and resins, too, for treating fever, sickness, or aching joints. This pot contains honey and pigeon dung – an excellent cure for kidney problems!

DO YOU HAVE ANY OTHER MEDICINES?

I have some mixtures that are made up by alchemists. But as well as medicines, I have other ways of treating an ill person. I believe that most illness is caused by a lack of balance between the body's four "humors." The humors – blood, yellow bile, black bile and phlegm – decide a person's health and personality. To get them back in balance, I often make a make a small cut to allow some blood to flow out.

WHAT SORT OF OPERATIONS HAVE YOU DONE?

After battles, I've removed shards of metal such as arrowheads. I've also done amputations. Patients have to be tied to the operating table to keep them still – my hemlock potion doesn't always keep them asleep for long enough to saw the limb off. Afterwards, I cauterize the wound with hot irons to seal it.

The Castle Banquet

Luckily the knight isn't badly injured. Suddenly a fanfare of trumpets echoes from the great hall. You leave the doctor and follow a procession of servants carrying large plates of food. Inside the hall, there are minstrels and entertainers in a gallery above the diners. One of them beckons to you. You run up to the gallery and talk to one of the performers.

WHAT KIND OF ENTERTAINMENT WILL THERE BE?

The minstrels sing and play while the diners eat. Then the jester will have a go at making everyone laugh. He tells jokes and even pokes fun at the baron. There will be dancers, jugglers, and more music between each course of food – and there will be at least ten courses!

WHAT MUSICAL INSTRUMENTS DO THE MINSTRELS PLAY?

They play a lute, a flute, a pipe, drums, and a fiddle. The lute is based on a type of instrument the Crusaders brought back all the way from Arabia. The player plucks the strings. The minstrels' songs are about courtly love and chivalry.

WHO IS SITTING AT THE HIGH TABLE?

The baron and his most important guests, including the bishop, are at the high table. These lords and ladies get a tablecloth of white linen, silver plates, and the best food! The man standing beside the baron is the cup-bearer. He serves and sips the baron's wine to check it isn't poisoned.

Setting Out with the Pilgrims

The banquet was spectacular, and you saw some unusual foods, including sheep's feet and roasted songbirds! But now it's over and it's time for you to leave the castle and make your way back into the town. As you cross the drawbridge, you find yourself among a group of people. They are about to set off on a pilgrimage. You ask one of the pilgrims about his journey.

WHERE ARE YOU ALL GOING?

We're setting off on the long pilgrimage to Canterbury – we're going to Thomas Becket's shrine. Becket was murdered in the Canterbury Cathedral over 100 years ago, and soon became a saint. I've heard that many people go to visit his shrine. A priest told me I should go – if I pray there and give thanks, then my sins will be forgiven. When I get there, I plan to buy a badge as a memento of my visit to show my friends when I get home.

WHO ELSE IS JOINING YOU?

Well, there's a shipwright… he heard that you can buy a bottle of Becket's blood. He's hoping it will cure his sickly wife. Then there is a wealthy mother who is taking her lame child to the shrine to be cured. A monk is going, too. He is hoping to sell prayer books to raise money for his monastery.

Pilgrims traveling to Canterbury, from one of the windows in the cathedral.

HOW WILL YOU GET THERE?

It's a very long journey, so we are riding horses. We are traveling in a group as protection against attack by robbers on the way. Like many pilgrims to Canterbury, we will make the last part of the journey on our knees. I am looking forward to seeing the huge cathedral, and touching Becket's holy shrine.

A pilgrim badge showing Thomas Becket's shrine.

Back to the Present

Your six hours are over. You go back to the narrow street, with the town walls and castle towers looming. There you step back through the door into the little room. You quickly change your clothes – and the door back to the 21st century reappears. You walk through, leaving the medieval town behind. You wonder what happened to the walled town and its castle. Did it survive? What became of the people?

THE SHRINE

You discover that the shrine of Thomas Becket remained a popular pilgrimage site until King Henry VIII destroyed it, in 1538. In the 1530s, Henry closed down nearly all the monasteries and convents in England, Ireland, and Wales. He took all the precious metals and jewels that had been left by pilgrims at Becket's shrine – 26 cartloads in all!

Silverware like this was seized by Henry VIII when he closed down the monasteries and convents.

THE PLAGUE

You check a history book to see what happened next in medieval Britain after your visit in 1294. You're horrified to discover that in the next century, the bubonic plague (or "Black Death") swept across Europe, spread by fleas on rats. Between 1347 and 1349, a third of all of Europeans died from this disease.

The ruins of Conwy Castle, in north Wales.

THE CASTLE

The baron's castle was Conwy Castle, in north Wales. It's still there today, although it now stands as an impressive ruin. You discover that most of the town's walls, along with its 21 towers, have survived too. You decide to go and visit one day!

29

Glossary

alchemist A person who believed they could make a single cure for all illnesses by mixing chemicals, as well as gold from cheap metals.

amputation The cutting off of an arm or leg.

armorer A person who makes plate armor.

bailiff Employed by the lord of the manor, the bailiff was in charge of the peasant laborers, the animals and the upkeep of the estate.

baron A wealthy and powerful noble who had control over a large area of land that was owned by the king.

cauterize To seal a wound by burning it.

chain mail A type of armor made from lots of small linked metal rings.

chivalry A traditional set of beliefs and ways of behaving that knights were expected to follow.

coat of arms A special design used to represent a noble family or guild.

doublet A close-fitting upper body garment worn by boys and men.

earl An important noble who was just below the king in social importance but was not necessarily wealthy.

glaive A weapon made out of a long pole with a single-edged blade at the end.

guild A group or association to which medieval workers with a certain type of skills belonged, such as a carpenters' guild or a wool merchants' guild.

guild master A guild member who was very skilled and who trained apprentices.

high table A table in a dining hall, often raised on a platform, for the most important people.

hose Men's tight fitting trousers, similar to modern woolen tights.

humors The four bodily fluids that medieval doctors thought affected how healthy a person was and how they behaved.

illuminator A person who paints small pictures and decorations on texts.

lance A long weapon with a pointed end.

leprosy A painful and infectious disease that damages the skin, muscles, and nerves.

mace A club-like weapon, often with spikes on the end that could get through armor.

mummer A medieval traveling actor who performed in comic plays.

page A young boy who served a nobleman while learning to be a knight.

pilgrim A person who travels to a holy place.

plate armor Armor made from steel or iron plates.

portcullis A grilled door that slides down to protect the main entrance to a castle.

pottage A thick soup or stew.

reeve A reeve was elected by the peasants to work for the bailiff.

scribe A person skilled in writing text, such as manuscripts, by hand.

shrine A holy place linked to a person or an item that was considered sacred.

stocks A wooden frame in which a person's feet, or arms and head, were locked as a punishment.

trencher A thin block made from wood or stale bread, used as a plate.

For More Information

WEBSITES

http://www.bbc.co.uk/history/interactive/timelines/british/index_embed.shtml
British History Timeline, an interactive timeline of British history. Search by year or event to explore what happened before, during, and after the Medieval period.

http://www.knightsandarmor.com
Information on knights, including their armor, chivalry, and the crusades.

http://medievaleurope.mrdonn.org/
Lots of detailed information on Medieval life, such as the sound made by Medieval musical instruments.

http://www.learner.org/interactives/middleages/feudal.html
Middle Ages – interactive information on aspects of Medieval life, such as the feudal system and clothing.

http://www.skiptoncastle.co.uk/
Information on a Medieval castle. Pages include its history and people, and there's a 3D castle plan.

http://www.castlewales.com/conwy.html
Information about and pictures of Conwy Castle in north Wales.

BOOKS

Horrible Histories: Measly Middle Ages by Terry Deary (Scholastic, 2011)
Knights (Knights and Castles) by Laura Durman (Franklin Watts, 2012)
Medieval Life (Eyewitness Project Books) (Dorling Kindersley, 2009)
Medieval Medicine (Medicine Through the Ages) by Nicola Barber (Raintree, 2012)
A Medieval Monastery (Spectacular Visual Guides) by Fiona Macdonald (Book House, 2013)
Siege (Knights and Castles) by Laura Durman (Franklin Watts, 2012)

Index